Business Acquisition

B. Vincent

Published by RWG Publishing, 2021.

BUSINESS ACQUISITION

First edition. June 16, 2021.

Written by B. Vincent.

Also by B. Vincent

Bridge Pages
Business Acquisition
Marketing Automation

Table of Contents

Business Acquisition

Hello, and welcome to this course on business acquisition. In this course, we're going to cover how to purchase and take over existing businesses. This course is divided into three modules. Module one introduces us to the business acquisition concept. Module two covers finding businesses, brokers, and lawyers. And module three shows us how to actually get funding for the acquisition. By the time this course is over, you'll know how to effectively find, fund, and acquire businesses. So without further ado, let's dive into the first module. Okay, guys, welcome to module one. In this module, our expert will introduce us to the business acquisition concept and give us a good layout of the land. So get ready to take some notes, and let's jump right in.

Module 1

So, buying a business sounds like an incredible proposition, it sounds maybe like something that's out of reach to your average person. However, you'll find during this course that it's actually a much more realistic idea than you may have previously thought, there's a whole lot of reasons why doing so, buying a business is actually more attractive to entrepreneurs than starting one from scratch.

So let's go over some of the reasons that you might want to buy a business instead of starting a new one. So the first thing that comes to mind is you get a revenue stream faster. okay, you literally become the owner of something that already is producing cash flow, bringing in money, you don't have to work up and slave to the point where you finally have positive cash flow coming in. So that's definitely a benefit, you could theoretically become the owner of a six-figure income stream, you know, within a matter of a week, if you pay for it. So that's one potential advantage. Buying a company is also potentially less risky because the business has already been proven to generate paying customers.

Now, that all assumes that the data that you see before you purchase is 100%, open and accurate, and nothing was withheld. So there obviously are a lot of risks with buying a business as well. But when you get down to those main numbers about market and audience and supply and demand and all that good stuff, there's a lot less risk involved, there's a lot less guessing and gambling involved, compared to what you would be doing if you were starting a business from scratch, and you didn't have that data, it's already historical, it's already proven when you purchase the business. There's less stress and work involved because the business is already up and running, it's already set up. So you don't need to create a launch strategy, you don't need to execute your launch campaigns, right? It's already beyond the startup stage.

Another benefit is hiring and recruiting, you really don't have to do them, you don't really have to do a whole lot other than perhaps bringing in a new manager to handle things for you, which we'll get to later. In most cases, the business will retain its employees, you get those as a package deal. Okay, so you're already getting people who know how the business operates, they know what they need to do to fulfill their job roles and keep it up and running. So you don't have to worry about the headache of hiring and vetting and recruiting and all that good stuff. Then there's systems are the lifeblood of a good and profitable business. And usually, you have to create those through a lot of trial and error systems like sourcing from suppliers and shipping and fulfillment and logistics and return policies and all these types of workflows. And if this, then, that all that stuff that you and your employees have to develop and come up with is sort of honed over time, well, that's already established, you don't have to worry about that.

And finally, buying a business, in many cases, is cheaper than building one. That sounds a little bit goofy, right? Because you see that giant price tag when you're buying a business. But if you're buying a business at the recommended level, which is we'll get to that in more detail later. But it's basically three times the net annual profit, you're getting a really, really good deal. For all the reasons above here, you're getting a great deal as far as time and effort. But you're also getting a great deal in terms of money. Because that business will be profitable within a very short amount of time to you, assuming you did your due diligence. And you're also getting all sorts of assets like the email list, the customer database, the code if you're buying a software app, for example. The brand, and all this other stuff, it's already included.

And again, because it already has cash flow, if you do the math, right, when you're coming up with the deal when you're negotiating, and you make that purchase, the financing that you acquire and the financing that you get for purchasing the business. So the loan, in other words, and in most cases, there's other options out there, and we'll discuss that later on. But that's canceled out by the cash flow already. So theoretically, it really doesn't cost you anything at all, if you're smart about it, and you get a really good deal. It's actually very similar to investing in homes, for the purpose of renting them out. Right, you might get a mortgage, for a home, let's say you do zero down, and you get a mortgage for $100,000, to buy a $100,000 home, and that sounds really expensive. Let's say your monthly cost for that home, both the mortgage and the utilities and the maintenance, let's say it comes up to about 13 $100 per month. Well, you have a tenant paying you rent at 15 $100 per month. So you've got $200 of cash flow, and more importantly, though, all those costs associated with it, including the mortgage, the $100,000 mortgage, well, that's all canceled out, it's all paid for by your tenant, so you're not actually paying anything. That's the perfect ideal scenario where you don't have to worry about, you know, other issues that get thrown into the mix.

But generally speaking, the math works out that way. What sounds like a huge investment, and a huge price tag and is, you know, these are real dollars, we don't want to belittle that. But what sounded like something massive, is actually largely canceled out by the cash flow. That's again, assuming that you acquired a good business, and you've got a good deal. So how do you make sure that that's the case? How do you make sure that you get a good business, and that you get a really good deal? Well, the first thing you want to consider is to surround yourself with experts, trustworthy advisors, the first person that you probably want to reach out to would-be an experienced attorney. Their job is to protect your interests and make sure that you're getting a legit deal. Their job is not the economics and the math of it. That's not their job is to figure out the cash flow and the income and the expenses and all that good stuff. That's your job and the job of other experts who you might enlist.

But the attorney's job is specifically to ensure that the deal is totally legit and that you are protected. Other experts that you can bring onboard include bankers, accountants, business brokers, people who specialize specifically in acquiring businesses and estimating their value and their payoff, so these guys can figure out what the expected income is going to be whether or not the claims that were made by the seller are accurate. They can figure out industry trends, they can figure out laws that might apply to the business, they can help you understand current market conditions. And whether or not the deal is actually going to work out in your favor.

Now one of the most important things for you and that team of experts that you surround yourself with, to do before you actually sign a deal is to dig deep into the business's history and finances. Right, before you seriously consider actually making that purchase. You want to find out as much as you can beyond sort of the storefront of stuff, you know, these businesses that are for sale will sometimes slap up a few figures, you know, regarding their cash flow, their income, their expenses, their traffic, you know, sometimes it might be a nice snapshot of the last three months. And it could be the case that they took some type of proactive action to make those three months as good as they are. But that regular operations outside of that snapshot aren't quite as impressive, let's say, and then that's a very real possibility. So you want to get in there you want to find copies of their certified financial records, you want to get their balance sheets, their cash flow statements, you know, you want to get their employee files including benefits, employee contracts, details on their employees, accounts payable, accounts receivable, any major leases, any major contracts that they have, and also dig into their legal history for past lawsuits and issues like that.

So you want to get your hands into all of that stuff or have the people who are on your team helping you do that. Get their hands into all that stuff and make sure everything is nice and clean. And be advised when you dig in, you might find, you know, some blemishes you might find that things aren't as rosy and that doesn't necessarily mean that you don't want the deal. In many cases I mean, you got to understand there's a reason people sell businesses, you know, it's not necessarily because everything's going perfect. Sometimes everything is going perfect, and the person just doesn't feel like running the business anymore. They just want to retire and go live on the beach, you know, with a good chunk of cash in their pocket, and that's fine. But in many cases, there's other aspects to the business that makes them want to sell it.

And that's not necessarily a bad thing, so don't get spooked if you see that things are not as rosy when you finally dig in deep into the data, you just need to assess how big of a deal each thing is, and whether or not it's something that you can improve upon. Because if you're buying a business, it's likely that you already had sort of a turnaround mentality, a fix, and flip mentality, they might have a tremendous product, but it turns out, you know, sales are down because their marketing sucks, and you're really good at marketing, you know. So it's not necessarily looking for these signs of something, you know, being less than perfect in the business and saying, at that point, you know, what, never mind we're not buying again, expect to find things like that. What you really need to do is when you find those things, you need to calculate and determine whether or not those are things you're confident that you can improve upon.

So what are some criteria for a good business acquisition? Well, the first one probably is cash flow. And specifically cash flow versus assets. Now a lot of people go out there, and they shop businesses because they want to acquire those assets. And assets are great, but you should prioritize cash flow. Remember, assets are things that by their very nature usually depreciate, okay, that doesn't mean they're bad. But it means that your focus really should be on cash flow because cash flow does not depreciate and of itself. Cash flow determines your ability to remain profitable and to pay off the financing that you use to purchase the business in the first place. That should be the first thing that you look at.

Another thing to look at is a business that remains afloat in spite of bad management, or in spite of some other negative aspect of it. So that means a business that continues to make money despite the fact that maybe the owner is not super business savvy, or is not good at what they're doing. Maybe they have bad service, maybe they have bad customer reviews, ironically, in a certain scenario might actually be a good thing. When you're shopping around bad customer reviews on a business that's still doing well means that that's an area for improvement. And that worst-case scenario, if your customer service was terrible, the business would still stay afloat, it's an indicator of how much demand there is, for the thing that's being sold, because of a business is still doing well, despite the fact that you know, it has negative reviews about bad customer support, if it's still doing well, in spite of that, well, that's a good sign that the business, that the thing that's being sold rather, is something that customers want. And that sets an incredibly important indicator, you can come in and solve the customer service problem, you can come in and solve the reputation problem, right? But what you know is that you have something that people want, and they want it enough that they still buy despite that negative aspect of the business, that's a really good sign.

They also want to find a business that can be managed and run with relatively low skills. Okay, you're looking for a business that is really simple. It sells something to a market that wants what it's selling. That's the meat and potatoes of the business that you're looking for. You don't want something that's super complex, at least not for your first business acquisition. You don't want to buy something, you know, like an engineering company or technology or science company, unless those are areas of your personal expertise, of course, or a law firm or something along those lines that require large amounts of investment in super highly technical skills or technical training for the employees or for the manager, you want to keep it nice and simple. And in a similar vein, you want to make sure it's something that can be easily run by someone other than you, right? Something nice and simple, where you get a manager to manage it for you, or a primary service provider to provide the service for you. Right, so let's say you've got a restaurant where you want to hire a good restaurant manager and a good chef. If you've got those two people, you'll be in good shape, right? You're looking for that type of scenario, okay, you're buying a hair salon, get yourself someone who's good at doing hair, and put them in charge of the operation. If you can find a business where it's easy to do that to just install a driver who's good at running the day-to-day operations, that would be ideal. So that's the type of business that you want to look for.

Now, let's talk about the actual money and math question. Generally speaking, you want to look to acquire a business that is selling for three times its annual net profit, approximately. Now, during the negotiations, there's obviously the opportunity, and you should attempt to bring them down further in price, the further below that critical marker of three times their net profit, the better because you've got more wiggle room there, you're able to pay off your financing and faster, you become profitable faster, more cash flow to work with and all that good stuff. But generally speaking, the starting point should be approximately three times their annual net profit. So let's say you're acquiring a business, let's say it's a used car dealership. And let's say they've got $500,000 in annual revenue, and half of that is profit, so $250,000 in profit. So the ideal price that you would want to pay for that business or that you wouldn't want to pay anything higher than would be $750,000. Okay, that would be the starting point, that should be where the negotiations begin, somewhere around that point. If you do that, it'll be much easier to maintain a good cash flow situation, much easier to pay off the financing, the loans that you used to purchase to make that $750,000 purchase, to pay back investors, make sure they get their money back, if you got a circle of investors to help you. With that purchase, everything becomes much easier if you can stay at or below that three times their net profit purchase price.

So those are just some general guidelines for what to look for when you're purchasing a business and to figure out if it's the right thing for you. In the next lesson, we're going to go over actually finding these businesses as well as tracking down the team of experts, especially brokers and lawyers to help you in your first business acquisition.

Module 2

Hey, folks, welcome to module two. In this module, our expert will go over finding businesses, brokers, and lawyers. So get ready to take some notes, and let's jump right in.

Alright, so we're going to start here on sort of the lower end of business buying and selling marketplaces. And by low end, all I mean is the average price tag and size of the business and all that we're starting here at the exchange, which is at exchange marketplace.com. And this is created by Shopify and Shopify, if you don't know who they are, they're sort of the premier online e-commerce store building platform. A very popular, huge, a huge percentage of the e-commerce stores online are created through Shopify, and they create a marketplace here where people can buy and sell businesses. And the cool thing about this marketplace here is that the data is directly fed from Shopify itself. So Shopify is able to actually validate and verify the sales and traffic data here. So there's no room for the business owners who are selling these to sort of fudge the statistics.

Now, it's not possible, really, for Shopify to verify what their expenses are as far as going out and buying, you know, paid advertising and stuff. So you still have to do your due diligence and stuff. But it is kind of nice to know that the numbers that you see here are directly from Shopify itself. Let's have a look at this one here, eco fish tackle looks like a very cool, business, environmentally friendly, all that good stuff, and they have some good numbers here. So right here, their average revenue per month is 34,000, their average sessions per month 66,000. So they're getting a whole lot of traffic, average profit is 11,000 per month.

Now, that actually would be a pretty good deal, 11,000, let's go ahead and grab our calculator here. That would give us times 12, an annual profit of 132,000. And of course, this time three was that sort of sweet spot number that we talked about earlier. So annual profit times three is generally where you want the sale price to be. So times three would bring us up to $396,000. And they're selling it for 79,000.

Now, why is that? Well, there could be a few reasons. The main reason though, is that like I said earlier, this is sort of the lower end or the in the small pond of places to buy and sell businesses, a lot of these Shopify stores don't actually have enough data to back up this number with a whole lot of certain A lot of these Shopify stores are created by people who create e-commerce stores. And they're good stores, but they run them for about, you know, six months or so. And in fact, here's a chart we'll have a look at in a second. And then they use those numbers, and they know it's an integrity thing, they know that they can go for the standard, you know, month times 12 times three price tag model here, at least not in good conscience, because they don't actually have that much proof of performance. They only have, you know, in many cases, several months of performance here. So you can read here about the business a little bit, why I was started, the reason for selling what's involved and running it. Most of these e-commerce stores are largely hands-off, all you're doing is maintaining ads that send traffic to them. And you've got maybe a virtual assistant who does the fulfillment and customer service and all that good stuff. Here's some more stats, we saw these ones already 30% profit margin average sales per month, 7000, that's units being sold, average revenue sales number would be 34,000. As we already saw, and here's the actual data that you want to look at. So clearly, this site was largely dormant and not used for several months, and then they started ramping it up and bringing in all those sales here. And you kind of have to make a, you know, a decision whether or not you want to pursue a store with such a short sales history.

However, that's kind of the whole point of the Shopify scene. And that's also why the price is so low compared to their average profit. Again, if they actually stuck to the standard model, and they had more history, you'd be paying something closer to this. And in this case, the price is much, much lower, but you can look into this company as much as you want to via the Shopify data here. And it might be a good jumping-off point for inquiring a little bit further asking more questions with the seller and having a business broker reach out to this company and get some more data. But that's what you can expect from the exchange from the Shopify marketplace.

Next, and stepping it up a notch as far as size and price tag is Empire Flippers. Empire Flippers is a very big database, compared to the exchange at least, as far as having large businesses, you know, legit businesses with, you know, longer sales history and that sort of thing. You can search Empire Flippers, the marketplace here, you'll notice a lot of these businesses have what are clearly the more standard profit, annual profit times three model year for their pricing. And there's a whole large spectrum of categories that these businesses exist in, we could click on, let's say, this one here, apparel and accessories is the niche is a SAS. And I've got some other monetization tags there, the price is 1,800,000. Or more than that, and the monthly net profit is at 52,000, with a multiple of 36x. So we can do, click on this one, and have a look at some more of the details for this listing. Empire Flippers is kind of a more serious site. So to unlock the actual identity, and more of the details about the listing, depending on their setting, you will actually be expected to provide some identifying information about yourself. And the main reason for that is companies don't necessarily want the fact that they are going to be selling soon or even toying with the idea of selling to the public, because sometimes that can negatively impact their business. Even if they're not selling for a bad reason. They're just selling because they want to retire, hearing the business is about to be sold sometimes can have a negative impact on their business. So that's the reason for the sort of secrecy here if you will. There's a whole lot of data here. It's quite a bit, you know, meteor than what we saw on the exchange. This is basically a SAS application, it's a plugin or an extension, that helps people sell products on e-commerce stores, and their primary source of revenue is through sale of products through this app. Okay, so it installs into the Shopify platform. It's one of the apps that you can get inside of Shopify. And when products are sold using this app, they get some revenue from that, and that's 97% of their earnings. And they also have a smaller percentage from different premium versions of the app, as well as affiliate offers. And it says youtube AdSense accounts, this is actually a pretty attractive model here because they don't have to spend a whole bunch on ads to get these specific sales that cause 90% of their revenue. All they're doing is advertising and spreading the word to get people to download the free app, and then they get that money, you know, as people sell through that app. So this is actually attractive from a buyer's perspective. They've got their traffic channels all laid out here, they talk about their expenses for, paid Facebook ads, shipping, they've got virtual assistant employees in the Philippines who handle the day to day running of the business, which also fits some of our criteria, it's going to be easy to plug in as an owner of this and have it run, you can go hands-on if you want to, or hire a manager to manage these virtual assistants. Let's see here, developers needed for approximately two to three hours a month to fix any bugs that's comforting.

So there's lots of lots of good information here. And this, this business in particular that we look at happens to fit a bunch of those ideal characteristics for business that you might want to inquire a little bit further about. So all the things that are included in the sale, these are the assets, you get the domain, all the site content, the trademark, the email list of 20,000 subscribers, which is absolute gold, Facebook account with 14,000 likes, I don't know how valuable that is anymore. We've got over that group with 51,000 members that is valuable as far as to reach on Facebook, YouTube accounts, 33,000 subscribers. So that's good, standard operating procedures, established supplier contracts and relationships, employee contracts. And they do note that you need to have an approved AdSense account, before purchasing the business to ensure a successful migration of the business. And this is another cool feature on Empire Flippers. They actually have podcast interviews here. So you can click here and listen for, how long is this one, 18 minutes of interviewing the owners of this business, and then sort of telling the story about it. So Empire Flippers is a very, very good place to shop businesses. The fact that it has so much great data doesn't mean that you shouldn't do your due diligence. But it does mean that there's a lot more information at your fingertips, and you can make a better decision about which businesses are worth time looking into or having a broker look into on your behalf.

The next one, this is probably the most common or most heard of one. And that's Flippa flippa.com, flippa.com back in the day, used to mainly be associated with buying and selling domains. And now they sell you know, entire businesses and apps here as well. And it's, it's got quite a bit of information, it's come a long way in the last few years. Let's click on this one right here, strobe prompts.com. And so far, we've been looking at pretty much only online stuff in a moment, we'll have a look at buying brick and mortar businesses as well. [Inaudible 28:40] business, the asking price is $305,000, and they literally do fake money. That's what this business is: it's a prop money business. And what they sell is very cool, very real-looking bundles of cash, for movies, for Hollywood movies, music videos, all that kind of stuff. I hear most of that stuff that you see people swimming in, in, in music videos, you know, when the rappers are throwing the money all over themselves and stuff, that's from companies like this. And so this is a pretty cool, unique company, I should say. And it looks like they have a net profit of $10,000 per month. So that would put them at about 120,000 per year. And 120,000 times three would be 360,000. So they're already offering a pretty low price here for this company. And, you know, there's less in the way of verification here versus, you know, Shopify, for example, the exchange that we were looking at earlier. So when you're dealing with a site like this, you're really really limited. It's beyond question if you're new to buying businesses. If you hire a broker and dig in and find the actual data, here, you've got financials with revenue and profit, here, big spike back in February. And that spike contributes to that average net profit per month you know.

So if that spike doesn't happen every year, you're not necessarily going to get that average net profit. And it would be very important to figure out what caused that spike, okay, was an exceptional month, what wouldn't, you need to know why that spike happened there and then get a real feel for what you can actually expect the net profit to be not necessarily the average, over a period of time that included an exceptional moment, for some reason in February, because this could have just been them getting lucky and having, you know, one big sale to a movie production company, you know, whereas this is the more average, you know, type of profit that they're usually seeing per month. So you really want to do your due diligence here. But Flippa is a great place to actually get out there and find lots and lots of businesses for sale. And now let's move to physical businesses. So BizBuySell is a great place to find actual brick-and-mortar local businesses. This is the real deal you're getting into big major purchases and acquisitions here. Lets go ahead and hit search here and have a look in the Florida area. Just sort of peruse, you'll see, since you're dealing with real physical brick and mortar businesses, the prices are considerably higher, as you can see. And we'll go over, you know how to deal with that in the funding lesson shortly here. But just one thing to be aware of is these prices are higher. And they're considerably higher than the standard annual revenue or annual profit, excuse me, times three model. And the reason for that is because they are bigger businesses, they're more real, at least in the sense of being tangible. And they have more history, in most cases, much more sales history, so they can charge a higher price. So as soon as you step out of the online into the physical space, there's a good chance you're going to see significantly higher prices, versus their annual average profit. So this one for example, here we have a chicken coop rental manufacturing and e-commerce retail business, located in Tampa, Florida. To purchase this, you would have to pay 11,500,000 their cash flow, however, is 2.6 million. 2.6 million times three is not 11.5 point 2.6 million times three is more like 7.5 million, somewhere between seven and 8 million is what that would end up being. So they're able to add a whole nother, this is probably closer here to you know, annual profit times four. So you know, there's a different math going on here. Because these are older, they can charge, you know, four or five times their annual profit because they have more data, you know, backing it up here, let's actually click here and look at the chicken coop company.

So asking price 11.5, we saw their gross revenue every year is 8.5 million. And they mentioned here that they have 376% year-over-year profit growth. And they grow through franchising. So that's pretty impressive. They've got let's see here, six years actually eight years in business, and six years ago is when they upgraded to actually doing manufacturing. And gives you all sorts of data about the stuff that they sell, including renting out their stuff here, lots, lots and lots and lots of information here about the business and what you can expect. Let's see they've got 100%, year over year sales, growth, and 376% in profit, growth, those are all good signs here. This looks like it would be a real, you know, serious company to look into investing in, you've got 12 employees that you would be acquiring with the business assuming that you're acquiring the employees, it's usually the case, but you want to make sure that that's actually part of the deal.

And then you've got the ability to contact the seller directly here. And this guy here, Ron is probably a broker, can be entirely certain but he's probably you know, it's kind of like buying real estate, right, the listing agent. This is probably a guy who specializes in selling businesses and he's doing that on behalf of these folks in Tampa. And that's who you would be communicating with. It's a really, really good idea to get yourself a business broker, especially for your first several times buying businesses. If you have not done it before, you can also access a more detailed valuation report here, and you can customize it as well. And this is, you know, it's a high ticket scene here, purchasing these businesses it's, it's a lot less of the recreational browsing going on. So you do have to actually pay for the reports if you want the super-duper in-depth details from BizBuySell here, but as you can see that the price isn't super high. These are like, you know, anywhere from 20 to 60 bucks for buying these reports. But these are your options, okay, for buying businesses online and buying businesses offline. This is where you start your shopping, theoretically. And then if you want to take it to the next step, that's when you need to move into finding actual brokers, people who are actually good at this and understand everything about it and will represent you and help you with your business purchases.

So let's talk about where to find them. There's a couple of ways, first off the marketplaces like this, and like Flippa and Empire Flippers, they actually have their own partnerships with brokerage companies. Okay, so BizBuySell you can actually find an entire listing here of brokers who specialize in this fact, we just saw this guy not too long ago, so we know he's active on the site. You can contact these people directly. They've got some information about their performance and their history. Thomas here has got over 10,000 businesses that he has sold help people sell. And here's all these services. This will be one place to find a broker and reach out to someone so you can work with them. Digital exits is another brokerage company. These guys are primarily servicing sellers, but they have listings where you can purchase and you know that you're going through a brokerage company rather than just sort of a for sale by owner situation. And it's kind of the same story over here at FE international. They help people buy and sell companies as well. They use the word website here, presumably because it's primarily SAS and e-commerce and online businesses. But this is another brokerage company that you could work with. They've had listings here for businesses, so having a broker involved is, generally speaking, going to be a good idea if you're new to buying businesses.

But perhaps even more important, the broker would be an attorney. You want to have an attorney on your team advocating for you and then you know, looking out for your best interest. AVO is a great place to find an attorney to find a business attorney specifically. Let's go through here, go to business attorneys, and choose your state let's stick with Florida just as we were using that example earlier and in the state of Florida, we've got tons of people that your scroll through these the ones that say add next to them, of course, means that they have paid to be featured towards the top. And in the case of these two guys, we've got one review each. You want to look for people with lots of reviews and lots of experience under their belt for business law. So, Jacqueline here if we were to click on her 185 reviews, that's pretty stellar. And we can read a little bit more about the services that she provides. What her experience is, does look like she's mostly in the real estate area there which is not a bad thing she probably has a very wide experience. But businesses, only 10% as far as how she ranks herself and the percentage of her practice, her history of practice.

We've got Kevin Durant ski here specifically mentions buying, selling, or starting a business. So that might be a lead to follow up on here and see if it's worth reaching out to this gentleman. See we've got business makes up 25% of his expertise so this might be someone to reach out to. And it's always good to vet your lawyers and figure out if they are as good as they say that they are on the listing sites, right? Martin Dale, which is a very cool tool for looking up lawyers and seeing how they're rated by their peers and that sort of thing. So, these guys have a whole lot of information, a very large database on lawyers in the United States, and let's just look up, Bob here, for example, and you've got all these individuals here. Click on their profiles and you'll see peer reviews, these are instances in which they have been reviewed by other lawyers, other people in their industry, got biography, you've got areas of practice, you've got, in some cases it doesn't have it here but in some cases, you'd actually have cases that they've been involved in listed here, education history, all that good stuff admission to the bar. And then of course the peer reviews here. And as you can see this guy looks pretty stellar.

So, this is always a good idea when you're hiring an attorney, you're not looking to nitpick too much, these are attorneys, and you're not, so you're just looking to make sure that there isn't anything particularly troubling that stands out about an attorney that would make you want to maybe think twice and then keep shopping for another one. So this is it, this is where you start your shopping for businesses. This is where you know, figure out who you might want to look into and consider purchasing from obviously leverage brokers and make sure you've got a lawyer in tow if you embark on this business buying journey, okay? And the next big question of course is funding, how do you purchase businesses with such high price tags, especially if you don't have a whole lot of capital on hand yourself, and we'll cover that in the next module.

Module 3

Alright, welcome to module three. In this module, our expert would show you how to actually get funding for your business acquisition. So get ready to take some notes, and let's jump right in.

Alright, so this will be a pretty straightforward and quick lesson, we're just going to go over the various funding options for a business acquisition. Now, the options are many, there are so many ways to fund your business acquisition. We're going to start with traditional banks, you'll notice they usually try to offer you two different options. One is their own product, so their own actual traditional bank loan in house, and the other is an SBA loan if you're in the United States, and an SBA loan is this, not a loan from the SBA it's not from the government, but it's backed by the government. Okay, and banks are usually more comfortable doing that because there's a government-backed loan. And for you, it's kind of a win, because the interest rates on SBA loans tend to be considerably lower and other terms are better as well, you know, longer repayment terms, shorter monthly payments, smaller monthly payments, I should say. So an SBA loan is great traditional bank loans can also be attractive depending on your credit so if you've got a credit score of, let's say 700 plus, there's a good chance banks are going to be interested in speaking to you about a traditional in the house, bank loan, they're their own product.

They're also, however, going to want to see a lot of financials and history about the business to make sure that the business actually is viable, okay? There's also sometimes an expectation that you have industry experience, okay in that particular area of business for the business that you're purchasing. You might not think that you need that experience and you might be able to make to them, the case that hey look, I'm hiring a manager who has that experience, but it's going to be one of those factors that might work against you if you don't personally have that experience. So you've got to make your case and ultimately just see what they offer you. The other option here would be credit union loans, now credit unions are technically nonprofit. Basically like banks but they're not technically banks, they're nonprofit institutions, and the members actually own and control them. And, you'll often find that they have lower interest rates and lower fees than your traditional banks and that their lending requirements are going to be a little bit more flexible.

And the other cool thing about credit unions, is they're a little bit more human. Some people put it that way: they're a little bit more human, a little bit more personal. I mean you can actually make a more, you know, human to human case about why you think the business will succeed, you know hey I've bought businesses before or I've owned a business before, or I'm bringing on a great manager that sort of thing, things like that that oftentimes are hard to, you know, hard to push those ideas through to a traditional bank because a traditional bank has very rigid templates of requirements. A credit union is usually going to be a little bit more likely to sort of listen to what you have to say and take those different variables into consideration. Does that kind of make sense? There are obviously eligibility issues with credit unions. Most credit unions cater towards a specific group of people, so there's a military credit union, there's a credit union for people who go to a particular school that sort of thing. So obviously, look into what you might be eligible for and, you know, reach out to credit unions and then see what their offer is versus a traditional bank, but another one and this is a more recent one, are these newer online business loans, okay these newer companies that are just offering applications you probably see ads for them all the time if you've been in business for a while, you know, a cabbage fund the box funding circle, these are all online business loans, and there's some, some definite pros and cons here. The application process is super streamlined. It's very quick, very easy to get a yes or no to get your information in their type it up, you know take five or 10 minutes going through an application process and get a yes or no, relatively quickly. However, the interest rates are kind of all over the place, okay.

Sometimes you'll find relatively low interest rates, but a lot of times you'll find really high-interest rates. So obviously there's a lot of factors that go into consideration with your interest rate, but just know that there's, there's, there's not a really tight shot group with the interest rates for these online business lenders, these non-traditional lenders. So you can see a very low one in one case and a very high one in another case, but these tend to be really quick, easy, and convenient for you to be able to shop around a whole lot. And, you know, apply to several of them, and compare interest rates, and they do sometimes have higher interest rates than traditional banks. The other option is online, personal loans, you can get funds through an online personal loan theoretically and use that for business you have to be really careful here, this is, this is not super advisable you really want to pay close attention to the terms and see how much the bank cares about what the money is used for some of them, probably most of them are very clear that the funds are not to be used for business. So you want to make sure that you're operating, you know, in a compliant manner, with, with these loans, but it is something to theoretically look into and speak to those lenders about another one that isn't talked about as often if you own your home and you have for a while, you actually have significant equity in your home would be a home equity line of credit. So, in this case, the interest rates will usually be super low compared to your more traditional loans, the terms will be longer, the payments will be easier, which is really important stretching your payments, your monthly payments are really important in those early days of acquiring a business, you know. And the other cool thing is it's also tax-deductible. Okay, the interest, at least that you pay on your home equity line of credit is tax-deductible, so that's another great benefit to consider. The downside here obviously is that you are using your home, the place that you live as collateral, right? Which a lot of people might not be comfortable with, but it's pretty easy to qualify for these low-interest rates and easy payments. It's a comfortable loan to have if you have that equity in your home and if you're comfortable with, you know, using the place that you live as collateral in case you know the business doesn't end up working out, you know, you know that they're going to end up coming after your home, obviously.

Another option and this is pretty common is seller financing, the seller financing, literally means you're just coming up with a payment plan or installment plan with the actual owner, and the owner essentially acts as the lender, in this case. This really depends on the personal circumstances of the seller. In many cases, you'll find sellers who, the whole reason they're selling is because they want that lump sum and they want to go retire on the beach, right? So that they might not be interested in this, but many of them, it's more important that they just go hands-off, they're not interested in running the business anymore. And they're okay with just being paid for the business over time so they might be open to seller financing, and in many cases is actually a win-win for both of you. In some cases, so depending on the circumstances, it might be a good option to have the seller finance the loan, you'll often get more flexible terms from the seller because they understand the situation a little bit better. So you might get the luxury of paying more easily as you go. And this could result in, you know, an easier time managing your cash flow, managing your budget, that sort of thing, but the big thing here is you still want to treat it as seriously as a traditional loan. And because this is a person-to-person agreement sort of between you and the seller, you're going to have to bring in your own lawyer to draft up the contract. Okay, or if they draft up the contract of course you'll want to have a lawyer of your own review it and make sure that it's all very clear and airtight if you engage in this. But this can be really advantageous for both of you if you decide to go this route, depending on your circumstances and their circumstances.

And finally, there's the investor approach. Now investors could be your friends and family could be actual venture capitalists folks, you know, angel investors, that there are a lot of people who like investing in business acquisitions, okay? It's actually much less risky to invest in the acquisition of an existing business that has history and has proof that's actually working in an up and running, than it is to invest in a startup for obvious reasons, right? So, many of those same people who you would go to if you were starting up. Okay, if you have local angel investors, and then those organizations and those meeting meetings and meetups do in fact exist. Many times you can pitch to them, a business acquisition, and there'll be all yours. You know, it might not be as exciting as a brand new startup, you know, getting in on the ground floor and seeing those high returns on investment. But those are also super risky and much less likely to succeed. So for a lot of these investors, they'll see a business acquisition as one of the less risky and more foolproof investments that they can make, and then they have a higher likelihood of seeing a return on their investment.

So there's this: this realm of funding is not something that you should ignore, you know, mostly because you can actually use a combination of funding right if you could have, let's say you're trying to acquire a business for $300,000. Well if you can have friends, family, and angel investors, take care of 100,000. Well, that means that the loan that you need is only 200,000. You've just decreased the burden of finding traditional lending by 1/3 because now you only need to convince a bank or a credit union, you know, or one of those online lenders to give you 200,000 instead of 300,000, right? So it's not necessarily picking one of these options it's it's trying to figure out how you can best accumulate the total amount that you need to purchase the business and that could end up being a little bit of loan a little bit of credit union, and a little bit of investing from friends, family or angel investors, you know, it could be a combination of those.

So, it's something where you really want to roll up your sleeves, look at all the options and reach out to a whole lot of different entities to see how you can best get that funding to acquire your business.

Don't miss out!

Visit the website below and you can sign up to receive emails whenever B. Vincent publishes a new book. There's no charge and no obligation.

https://books2read.com/r/B-A-QWUO-TGPPB

BOOKS 2 READ

Connecting independent readers to independent writers.

Also by B. Vincent

Affiliate Marketing
Affiliate Marketing
Affiliate Marketing

Standalone
Affiliate Recruiting
Business Layoffs & Firings
Business and Entrepreneur Guide
Business Remote Workforce
Career Transition
Project Management
Precision Targeting
Professional Development
Strategic Planning
Content Marketing
Imminent List Building
Getting Past GateKeepers
Banner Ads
Bookkeeping

Bridge Pages
Business Acquisition
Marketing Automation

About the Publisher

Accepting manuscripts in the most categories. We love to help people get their words available to the world.

Revival Waves of Glory focus is to provide more options to be published. We do traditional paperbacks, hardcovers, audio books and ebooks all over the world. A traditional royalty-based publisher that offers self-publishing options, Revival Waves provides a very author friendly and transparent publishing process, with President Bill Vincent involved in the full process of your book. Send us your manuscript and we will contact you as soon as possible.

Contact: Bill Vincent at rwgpublishing@yahoo.com www.rwgpublishing.com

www.ingramcontent.com/pod-product-compliance
Lightning Source LLC
Chambersburg PA
CBHW030535210326
41597CB00014B/1157